Marcus Meleton has appeared on GERALDO and the PLAYBOY CHANNEL and to date has been interviewed on over 100 radio stations across the USA, Canada, New Zealand, and Australia.

Here's What The Reviewers Had To Say:

"...laughed heartily at several points."

"I'd recommend it to any man who's ever wondered why a woman left him for a guy who was a jerk and to any woman who's wondered why she stayed with a jerk who treated her badly. In other words, about 85 percent of the human race."

"...a humerous answer to *THE HITE REPORT.*"
Phil Sanderlin
ATHENS OBSERVER

"...more often than not the truth hits home."
Jill Kleiss
COSTA MESA DAILY PILOT

"Marcus Meleton wrote **THE** book on nice guys."

"...whimsical, carries a thread of truth ...about women who choose the wrong man and stay with him, no matter how much it hurts."
Terry Goodrich
FORTH WORTH STAR-TELEGRAM

Also covered by USA TODAY, THE NATIONAL EXAMINER, ORANGE COUNTY REGISTER, LAS VEGAS SUN, DALLAS MORNING NEWS, and RADIO-TV INTERVIEW REPORT.

This book is available at special quantity discounts for sale, singles groups, promotions, premiums, or fund raising. For details write to:

Attn: Marketing Dept.
Sharkbait Press
P.O. Box 11300
Costa Mesa, CA 92627-0300
(714) 645-0139

NICE GUYS DON'T GET LAID

Marcus P. Meleton Jr.

PRESS

939 West 19th St. Suite E-1
Costa Mesa, CA 92627

ISBN 0-9635826-0-7
(Previously ISBN 1-55666-013-8)

Library of Congress Catalog Card Number 93-83581

Typeset by Lee Savoit Graphic Design

Sharkbait Press
P.O. Box 11300
Costa Mesa, CA 92627-0300
(714) 645-0139

Printed in the United States of America
10 9 8 7 6 5 4 3 2

ACKNOWLEDGEMENTS

It's gratifying to see what can be done for a book on a reprint. The difference between the limited first issue and this revised edition is like night and day. Thanks go to Sharkbait Press, for the care taken to do it right.

The result is some new material and an excellent print. But that change is not nearly as revolutionary as the change in society since the first edition. At that time, not getting laid was a major indication of rejection. Now with rampant sexually transmitted diseases and surprise pregnancies, the title is losing some of its negative qualities. Maybe a wave of responsibility will sweep the nation and this title will be perceived as a positive statement — if not the sign of a long and prosperous life. No matter what, one thing will always remain the same: Single Nice Guys will always be on the "Don't Get" side of the equation in relationships whether the measurement is dates or "scores."

I must thank the people who helped make this book possible. For the revision, Donna Felts provided the embarrassing realization of how poor my grammar remains. Thank you for reopening the scars that have been closed since the return of my last English assignment. Mary Lou Goforth was the person who encouraged and supported my determination to get a reprint and Harold Johnson did the final checkout, before typesetting. For the original print, thanks go to Jay Johnson, Jean Tohill, Mike Brenda, Orpha & Jake Valentine, Mark Adrian, and Randy Smith for their help and support.

To the dates who provided me material for this book, I give my undying gratitude. Apologies to those for whom I provided material.

TABLE OF CONTENTS

Illustrations by Edward Christopher

PROLOGUE

The Origin Of The Nice Guy Theory

It's 1984 and a party is raging. Graduation is at hand. It's late and I'm tired but the thought of finishing school has got me pumped. Life couldn't be better. Everything is great. Everything!! Everything, except for the fight that was to start outside. Don't get me wrong, a few beers and a good fight can be the sign of a healthy party, but this was different.

I, (Marcus), Johnston, Adrian, Mark, and Randy stumbled into the graduation party after my friends had decimated my liquor cabinet. There had been great concern on their part that moving the contents to my new job would be too great a task. With that potential problem alleviated, we are now in the middle of a high octane party, swearing to reunions and dredging up exaggerated recollections of seedy, embarrassing moments about each other. Absorbed as we are, it's hard to ignore him. His name slips me so I'll just call him the "Jerk".

The Jerk is far too drunk, even in our eyes. He circulates through the party, booming abuse at his girl friend and the hostesses. Finally he leaves, with his girl friend in tow. While following another couple out the door, the Jerk directs some of his crude remarks to the other man's date. A fight ensues. The Jerk's girl friend screams for help and the party empties onto the street with the five of us close behind.

The fight ends quickly. We arrive finding neither seriously hurt, but both bleeding. The man who defended his date is sitting on the curb as his date wipes the blood on his face. The Jerk was standing but clearly took the worst of it. He threw off all attempts by his girl friend and a growing number of women to settle him.

MARCUS: "Looks like we missed it."

ADRIAN: (Pointing at the Jerk) "That's the creep we saw at the party."

JOHNSTON: "He sure got his clock cleaned. I'm sorry I wasn't here for it."

JERK: (Yelling at his girl friend) "Get away from me you &%$# Bitch." He stomps toward us trying to shake the four women following him. His shirt is torn and hanging in pieces. His face is bleeding in several places.

JERK's GIRLFRIEND: "Please don't yell. Someone will call the police."

JERK: (Yelling at the windows of the buildings surrounding him) "They can call the *&%$$% Police if they want. I'll kick their &&%^$ ass." (Turning back to his girl friend) "Why don't you just shut the *&%$ up."

JOHNSTON: (Pointing at the JERK) "Hey bud, if YOU don't shut up, the police won't find anything left to kick."

MARCUS: "Not a bad idea Johnston, he still looks too pretty."

The Jerk, seeing several willing opponents looses interest. He does an about face and pushes through his entourage of women as they flash angry looks at us.

GIRL #1: (Glaring at us with her hand on her hip) "Stop causing trouble."

GIRL #2: "Can't you see he's hurt"? They walk off in a huff.

MARK: "Jeeze, you'd think we were the cause of this."

The Jerk finally submits to a drive to the emergency room. He continues to level verbal abuse at his girl friend, the hostess, and the other women as they pack him into their car. Another car starts to follow, then stops. One of the passengers remembers to retrieve the man who had defended his date.

ADRIAN: "Look!" (He gestures toward the cars pulling into the street) "He kills the party and the best-looking women leave with him. I guess we're supposed to learn something from this but it escapes me."

JOHNSTON: "We learned we should have kicked his ass while we had the chance."

MARCUS: "No, we learned that women are attracted to jerks."

JOHNSTON: "What the hell does that have to do with the party breaking up?"

MARCUS: "The Jerk starts a fight, ruins a party, and leaves with four women. We don't even have dates."

JOHNSTON: "Well, I didn't want to have a date tonight."

MARK: "Yeah. It must have been a long time since you've wanted one." (He smiles as he places an imaginary knife in Johnston's back.)

JOHNSTON: (Turning around) "You want to join that guy at the hospital!"

MARCUS: "Cut it out! ... What I said is true. The women you treat the worst are the ones you keep the longest."

JOHNSTON: "This isn't one of your stupid theories on life is it?"

MARCUS: "No. I'm just saying that the first thing you hear from a girl about to ditch you is 'I think you're a Nice Guy BUT ...'"

JOHNSTON: "This IS one of his stupid theories! You remember the one about how teachers have a plot to synchronize homework and tests to coincide."

MARK: "I kind of believe that one."

RANDY: "What about his theory that humans have eaten red meat, potato chips, and candy so long that we've evolved to where they are now dietary requirements."

ADRIAN: "Yeah. If the back-to-natural-foods trend continues, people are going to croak from lack of cholesterol, refined sugar, and salt coursing though their veins."

MARCUS: "I was just kidding."

JOHNSTON: "Yeah. Sure." (Everyone shakes their head)

MARCUS: "You better hope it's true. Most of you are following my diet plan, except you've added beer."

ADRIAN : "OK, Marcus. Lets hear this theory."

MARCUS: "It's simple. You tell me the things women look for in a man? What attracts them?"

RANDY: "Dependability. Loyalty."

JOHNSTON: "Romance. Flowers."

MARK: "I thought Johnston's idea of romance was a six-pack and tickets to professional wrestling."

JOHNSTON: "Well what do you think women like?"

MARK: "A guy with a future, a good job, and a little intelligence."

ADRIAN: "Johnston's got little intelligence." (Johnston grabs for Adrian's collar but Adrian slips free)

MARCUS: "Now, think back to the times when you were really impressed with a girl, when you became romantic, dependable, all those things you mentioned. Can you remember a woman that was overcome by it?"

ADRIAN: "No. I usually got dumped. But then I always get dumped."

JOHNSTON: "I don't know. I think it worked once. I usually got dumped though and it was for a jerk that couldn't hold a job."

MARK: "It almost worked for me once but then I sent her flowers. The next thing I know she went back to the old boy friend she used to complain about."

MARCUS: "OK, now tell me what professions are notorious for attracting women?"

ADRIAN: "Rock Stars."

JOHNSTON: "Pro Athletes."

MARK: "Politicians."

RANDY: "You've got something there, Marcus. Make it a doctoral thesis. You can title it something sophisticated like *NICE GUYS DON'T GET LAID*."

MARCUS: "Go ahead and laugh but it needs to be written. There's no way I can use that title though, my parents and grandmother would disown me."

JOHNSTON: "A book! Marcus is going to write a book on one of his stupid theories. That's the day. Let's go take the author out for some beer."

Is it a "stupid theory?" Let's see.

CHAPTER 1
Nice Guy Theory

DEFINITION: **NICE GUY** - *A term used by women to depict a male who is courteous, considerate, and dependable and therefore undesirable as a mate. (Syns: Gentleman, True Friend)*

Can this be true? Isn't it a woman's dream to have a nice guy who is steady, honest, loyal, and romantic? One who knows when to pay a sweet compliment and when to send flowers? A man who is strong but considerate, sensitive, and caring? An intelligent man who is responsible and trustworthy? Romance novels pull in fortunes displaying men with such qualities. So this must be what women want.

Well, isn't it?

WRONG!

DON'T CONFUSE MEN WOMEN DREAM ABOUT
WITH THE MEN WOMEN ATTACH THEMSELVES TO

Do romance novels sell because women latch onto honorable, kind, loving men and then double their pleasure by reading books mirroring their lives? Or is it more likely that women go after amorous, undependable, insensitive jerks and then buy romance novels by the truckload?

Have you ever heard the saying, "Nice Guys always get the girl?" Neither have I. Because there is no such saying. This can be illustrated by a few famous examples. Larry Hagman played a Nice Guy in the television show, *I Dream of Jeannie*. It wasn't until he began playing J.R. Ewing in *Dallas* that adoring letters began to stream in. John Derek marries and divorces Linda Evans and Ursula Andress, only to get Bo on the rebound and place her in porno movies. Most guys could have settled for any one of them, without the need to pimp their nude photos. Would you believe that Charlie Manson still receives adoring letters from women, some who were not even born during his heyday. This is true of Richard Ramirez and others like him. Sick isn't it? Are pickings really that slim? It's enough to send men to pathetic Wild Man gatherings, and men support groups.

What about complaints by women about such behavior? A multitude of books are written by women about jerks they date. Numerous Opra Winfrey shows focus on how awful men are. What they don't realize is that rather than being payback, it's actually a dedication to men who are successful at getting women. Look at the Kennedys. Did their reputation hold them back or **increase** their chances with women. Don't think for a second that it keeps women from voting for them. You need only look as far as President Clinton to understand this. Here was a chance for women to show disdain for a philanderer, instead his wife stands by his side and his election to the Presidency is primarily attributed to the women's vote.

Take another angle on this phenomenon. Why was there an intense interest in the television series *Beauty and the Beast*. A man who lives in the sewers with the face of a beast had women's hearts fluttering. Could you chose a more impossible relationship? But impossible may actually be desirable. Men for ages have complained that women who have spurned them suddenly show interest after they're married.

What professions are famous for magnetically attracting women? Let's take the obvious ones: Rock Musicians, Politicians, Actors, Pro Athletes, and Drug Dealers. A pretty sordid lot, don't you think? But always awash with women. Do these professions bring the word monogamous to mind, honesty, or how about dependable? Of course not, but these guys score at a rate that embarrasses the rest.

Generalities? Sure. You can't say all women fall for such men. They don't, but when was the last time you saw a crowd of women around a hard working accountant? Do college women congregate at the Engineering department or around the football and basketball players? In high school does the guy who is not a sports star, who treats women with respect, makes good grades, and sees little use for drugs have to fight women off? No! These are the Nice Guys. Their attraction is minimal. They're nice, but not dangerous. A girl's father even likes them.

Don't let the title of the book mislead you. It's not that a guy's ultimate goal is going to bed with a woman (although it ranks), it's just frustrating to watch some guys get women effortlessly. To see the women you would beg to take out to dinner practically rip off her cloths for a guy famous for being a disaster. Am I jealous. Not with my reputation. In the four short years of high school, I kissed at least two, maybe three girls right on the mouth. Bear with me, I know a little about Nice Guys.

CHAPTER 2

The Nice Guy Test

Are you a Nice Guy? Is your boyfriend a Nice Guy? The following test will put this book into perspective. If you are a man, what category of a man are you? The results of the test will give you insight into why women react to you the way they do.

If you are a woman, it is especially useful. You know the kind of man you dream about, the results will tell you what kind of man you go for. Apply it to your boyfriend or men to whom you are attracted by answering the questions yourself. If you are enthralled with the man, let a friend answer the questions for you. Your objectivity is questionable.

The test is multiple choice. Record your answers and evaluate the results using the instructions at the end.

NICE GUY TEST

1. How do you typically look when you arrive to pick up your date?
A. I wear my church clothes.
B. I like to dress up. Sometimes I bring a small present or flowers.
C. I dress casually unless I am very impressed with the woman.
D. I'm late, dress as I want, and if I bring anything it's a sixpack of beer.
E. I take a knife.

2. "Women are special." Is this statement true?
A. Yes. But they scare me.
B. Most Always.
C. Sometimes.
D. One or two, but only temporarily until I have my way with them. And I will have my way with them.
E. Only when tied and gagged.

3. Generally, when a girl cancels out of a date ...
A. NOT APPLICABLE. I don't get the date in the first place.
B. I get a weak excuse if I get one at all.
C. she says she is sorry and would like to make it another time.
D. she cries and begs for forgiveness. The only excuse I'll accept involves death (hers).
E. she moves, changes her name, and gets plastic surgery.

4. When I meet a girl, I ...
A. talk about Mother.
B. want to get to know her, find out who she is, and what she does.
C. want to get to know her but only if she is worth it.
D. I see a conquest in the making.
E. usually scare them off.

5. I think women are ...
A. like dear old mother.
B. should be put on a pedestal.
C. are fantastic sometimes.
D. good for only one thing.
E. the scourge of the earth.

6. A girl cancels a date, gives a feeble excuse, and in the process blows your weekend.

A. You cry.

B. You assume she told the truth and wanted to go with you.

C. You are disappointed but might try again.

D. It never occurs. If it did, there are others waiting in the aisles.

E. You set dynamite to her house.

7. On Valentine's Day ...

A. I get a card from Mom.

B. I send cards but receive few.

C. I get some cards and send a few.

D. I get a lot of cards and read only the ones I want. I send no cards unless it scores points I can collect on later.

E. I don't get any cards and I blame all women for it.

8. I get dates ...

A. through Mother.

B. through a great deal of effort, including groveling and expensive offerings.

C. easily sometimes and hard other times. My success runs hot and cold.

D. without effort. Many times they ask me.

E. if I pay for them to go. Sometimes that isn't enough.

9. When I am at a bar ...

A. I do not go to bars.

B. I rarely get anywhere with women.

C. I occasionally get a phone number.

D. I score frequently.

E. I drink till I pass out. Of course this is only if they let me in.

10. A girl I date for a long time quits seeing me because ...

A. I am boring.

B. I don't know why, many times it is for someone else.

C. we fight too much.

D. I told her to get lost, or she caught me fooling around.

E. I threatened her life.

11. When I settle down ...

A. I want someone to help me tie my shoes and dress me.
B. I want to get married and live like Ozzie and Harriet with lots of kids.
C. I might want to get married. Kids are a maybe.
D. I'll settle down when I am dead and buried.
E. I can't settle down. The world is after me.

12. Marriage ...

A. is for grownups.
B. is a pleasant way to spend a life.
C. might be nice.
D. is a mistake unless she is rich and beautiful and doesn't mind when I fool around.
E. is impossible.

13. If I ever got married I would ...

A. have to have Mother's approval.
B. be forever faithful.
C. be faithful, maybe.
D. be faithful at least the first week or until the first opportunity to score, whichever comes first.
E. lock her in a closet to keep her away from other men.

14. I get laid ...

A. What does "getting laid" mean?
B. at least once every two years, sometimes.
C. a few times a year.
D. I'm not sure how many times, but it's somewhere between 365 times a year and whatever my hero Wilt Chamberlain says is his yearly average.
E. never, but I get screwed a lot.

15. Look at your charge card bills. Those related to women are ...

A. mostly things I get for my mom.
B. for dinners, flowers, presents, plays, etc.
C. for sport events, dinner, concerts, occasionally flowers.
D. I never pay. If I do its to buy beer or tickets to professional wrestling or a tractor pull. Look on my date's credit card bill to see the places I take her.
E. for semi-automatic weapons.

Take your test results and grade it by giving each "A" answer 0 points, 1 point for "B", and so on up to 4 points for each answer of "E". Total your score and refer to the five groupings below.

Score 0-8   Mama's Boy

Move back home, if you aren't there already. You are looking for a girl like the girl that married dear old dad. Women like that don't exist and if they do they have no interest in you.

If a Mama's Boy gets married, it's usually to a husband beater. Due to rarity and hopelessness, this type will not be covered further in this book but it is suggested he read on. There is a lot of ground to cover.

If you are a woman and like this type of man, they are an easy kill. They're great if you want someone to control or abuse or if you want someone who won't possibly fool around on you. It is preferable that he has money or stands to gain from an inheritance. The negative side is that you will have to fight for the position with his mother, listen to his elephant jokes, and watch him read his subscription of Mad Magazine.

FAMOUS EXAMPLES - Felix Unger in The Odd Couple and Walter Mitty.

Score 9-22   Mr. Nice Guy

You poor sap. You are everything a girl thinks she wants but not what she is attracted to. Women chew you up and spit you out. You never get laid. At least you have this book dedicated to you.

If you are a woman and a guy you date rates as this type, you have it made. The problem is that there is no thrill of victory and little danger of loss that can keep him interesting. If you have a conscience, you feel bad when you inevitably dump him.

FAMOUS EXAMPLES - Harry Connick Jr., Bobby Ewing in Dallas, Tom Selleck, and Joel in the movie Risky Business.

Score 23-37   Mr. Average

Sometimes you're a Mr. Nice Guy and sometimes you aren't. It depends on the woman in question. For men of this type, it means you probably want what you can't get.

For women, if he is strongly attracted to you, he will do anything for you and behaves like Mr. Nice Guy. If he is not attracted to you, he will use you and act like Mr. Abuse.

Score 38-52   Mr. Abuse

Mr. Abuse is the most successful with women. He is the one who gives the least and gets the most. Rampant outbreaks of venereal disease can usually be controlled from this source. Cure him and you have cured the problem.

For women who seek such a man, he will ruin you, but the thrill of the chase, the desire to win over and conquer him intrigues you and makes your life worth living. Read on – you will learn a lot about Mr. Abuse.

FAMOUS EXAMPLES - Wilt Chamberlain, Mike Tyson, J. R. Ewing, John Derek, James Dean, Marlon Brando, Rob Lowe, Mickey O'Rourke, Jim Morrison, Pablo Picasso, and Teddy Kennedy.

Score 53-60   Mr. Psycho

You should be in jail.

If you are a woman and this man comes to your home, pull out your .44 Magnum, open the door, and let him make your day. Since Mr. Psycho is as rare as Mama's Boy, he too shall not be covered. If attracted to such a man, seek a doctor's help.

FAMOUS EXAMPLES - John Hinkley Jr., Woody Allen, Richard Speck, Richard Ramirez.

Now that the results are in, let's cover the three primary types of men to learn more about them.

CHAPTER 3
The Three Primary Male Types

I. Mr. Nice Guy

Mr. Nice guy is our protagonist, the subject of this book and the most pitiful form of the three types we will cover. This poor guy always respects and reveres women. He protects them and tries to be aware of their feelings. He's an excellent fill-in until a better challenge appears, makes a great friend, and even parents like him. He takes a girl to the nicest places, calls on her faithfully, and, when the time comes, serves as a starting block as the girl leaves him for someone who will do none of these things.

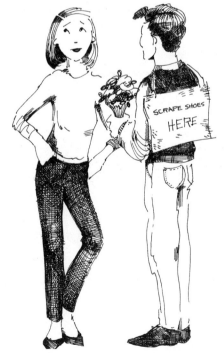

Mr. Nice Guy has awful bar manners. When he meets a girl, he actually makes an attempt to get to know her, find out where she's from, and what she does. Faced with a stable and easy mark, most women turn to stone and begin scoping out other prospects. Return conversation is at a minimum. Given the respect of a flattened highway opossum, Mr. Nice Guy gets embarrassed and scampers away with his tail between his legs. If the woman is charitable enough to accept a dance, it's to show others she's available.

Mr. Nice Guy is even worse at getting dates. In high school he could ask eight girls to the Prom and still not have a date. When he does get a date, it often doesn't pan out. Nothing can get in his date's way that might cause her to break the date, such as washing her hair, finger nail polish refusing to dry, or the anniversary of her parakeet's death. Nice Guys generally leave high school very inexperienced even in these times. Being a Nice Guy is the most effective form of birth control outside of castration (Though similar).

Following is a scenario of a not-too-infrequent occurrence in the life of Mr. Nice Guy.

Mr. Nice Guy - In Search Of A Date

NOTE: Diane's decision to go was based on two things, rejection by Mr Abuse (Shane) and the offer to see a play for free.

SHANE:
"Hey Babe, been thinking about you.
The Big Game is on the tube tonight.
How about you coming over and feeding me.
Grab a six-pack on the way. I'm all out."

NOTE: Shane had been thinking about her a total of five seconds
prior to making the call.

DIANE:
"Shane, you haven't called in so long. I've missed you. Luckily, I haven't anything special planned."

NOTE: Diane is right. To her, nothing *special* was planned.

III. THE SETTING: Two hours before the play opens.

MR. NICE GUY:
> "Diane, I just wanted to call and tell you
> I got reservations to La Restaurant."

DIANE:
> "I'm awfully sorry, but I can't make it at all tonight.
> Something important has come up."

MR. NICE GUY:
"Oh, I hope it isn't anything serious.
It's too bad, I was really looking forward to this."

DIANE:
"You're such a doll for understanding.
Maybe some other time."

NOTE: She called him a "*doll*." An object you play with and put in a box when you get bored with it. She didn't even bother to contrive a good excuse.

IV. THE SETTING: The Curtains Rise and the Play Begins.

NOTE: Shane has a grip on the two things he knows best.

NOTE: The rejection produces a fleeting thought of Mr. Nice Guy. That was the extent of Mr. Nice Guy's impact.

NOTE: He is obviously a Mr. Nice Guy. If he buys more tickets he will be Mr. Fool.

Being a Nice Guy does not mean the guy's a wimp. He's just a wimp around women. A particularly funny paradox involves women who have been through a very bad experience with a Mr. Abuse. At times they decide that all men should pay. Being an easy mark, it's Mr. Nice Guy who does most of the paying. His dates get canceled. He is accused when his intentions and conversation are misinterpreted because of her bad past experiences. His life's purpose seems to be buying all the meals and tickets that should have been bought by the Mr. Abuse in the past. Of course such gestures are considered repayment of a debt, rarely a compliment.

NICE GUY THEME SONGS:
Diary — Bread
Solitaire — The Carpenters
Wild Thing — Sam Kinnison version

II. Mr. Average

Mr. Average is not quite the sap Mr. Nice Guy is, but he does have his moments. He doesn't revere all women, only those he considers special. It's these *"special"* women he gets nowhere with. Those he does not consider special are the ones he does best with. This confuses him. Since his treatment of women varies, it gives Mr. Average a Dr. Jekyll, Mr. Hyde personality. Sometimes he is a Mr. Nice Guy. Sometimes he is a Mr. Abuse.

Although many women don't realize it, most men fall quickly for a woman. If they don't fall quickly, they most likely won't fall at all. When a Mr. Average falls, he becomes (GAG!) a Mr. Nice Guy. A Mr. Abuse falls for a woman but only on rare occasions. It primarily happens to Mr. Average. When it does, turn back to the section on Mr. Nice Guy to see the pathetic change that comes over him. When he does not care for a woman but she is interested in him, see the next male category for his description.

III. Mr. Abuse

The third type male is Mr. Abuse, the J.R. Ewing of man. (Also known as Mr. Abuse-them-and-leave-them). To him, women are good for only one thing. This makes him very successful as women seem to fall for his indifference, nonacceptance, and undependability. Of course not all women fall for this type, but enough do to keep him too busy to care about the rest.

His primary secret is an air of confidence with women. He could have zero confidence at anything else, no job, could be undependable, useless, and obnoxious. He could wear dresses at night and traipse around the house with the blinds down or wear an overcoat and shoes and visit school yards, but his inborn confidence with women overcomes all that. Whereas others have this confidence sporadically, giving them an up and down "love life," a Mr. Abuse always has it. Confidence draws women. When combined with a lack of conscience (the Genghis Khan effect), it is devastatingly effective.

How do you spot a Mr. Abuse? When he's pointed out, it's usually with the comment, "What does she see in him," or "Why does she go out with that S.O.B.," or "The only thing I hate about her is her boyfriend." He is the one you see at a party with the girl friend who is crying or the one that leaves his date alone while he puts the heavy hit on other prospects at the party. He accepts a *"NO!"* from a woman easily since he has no respect for her anyway, as opposed to a Mr. Nice Guy who takes the *"NO"* as a personal defeat. The only jokes he knows are those that insult women.

What is ironic is that Mr. Nice Guy seems to be most attracted to women who go out with Mr. Abuse. Mr. Abuse is the one a Mr. Nice Guy hears about when he consoles a girl over a guy that trashed her. Mr. Nice Guy identifies with her. He even hates the man for all the mean and awful things he has done and is then shocked when she goes back for more.

Mr. Abuse does well on a date. He gets a better response from a woman by taking her to McDonalds than Mr. Nice Guy does taking her to a candlelight dinner. A purchase of a box of Cracker Jacks does as much as roses from Mr. Nice Guy. In the long run Mr. Abuse always wins out and at much less cost and effort.

Mr. Abuse has excellent bar room etiquette. He gets obnoxiously drunk. Women come to talk to him while he acts indifferent and scopes out other "Chicks" and "Babes." If he makes an effort for a girl and gets brushed off, he doesn't get embarrassed like Mr. Nice Guy. He excuses himself with a statement like, "My mistake, in the dark I mistook you for good looking." She is immediately forgotten as he scopes out the next prospect, his ego fully intact. Many a N.O.W. woman was created by an involvement with a Mr. Abuse. Of course, the impact affects mainly Mr. Nice Guy since a Mr. Abuse has little time or desire to deal with one.

Many women fall blindly for Mr. Abuse. Almost all have fallen for him once. It seems that no matter what he does, a woman will be there to defend him and make excuses for him. Once a woman has fallen for a Mr. Abuse, she begins to speak a new language. Below is a translation guide to help decipher the truth from what she is saying. Women, take heed if you find yourself mindlessly spouting such comments.

Translation Guide For Women Dating A Mr. Abuse

SHE SAYS	INTERPRETATION
1. "He doesn't always act like this."	Just most of the time.
2. "When I'm alone with him he's different."	If he's like that in public who cares what he's like in private.
3. "I understand him."	She's the only one that doesn't.
4. "He doesn't treat me this way when we're alone."	When they're alone he treats her worse.
5. "He will change."	He will change when pigs grow wings and fly through hell wearing ice skates.
6. "We don't see each other more than twice a week. He wants his freedom."	He wants or is getting something on the side.

7.	"He is actually very sensitive."	His sensitivity is only to his own needs. Hers are irrelevant.
8.	"He apologizes for what he does and really is sorry."	Then he does it again.
9.	"All my friends hate him."	They do and they should.
10.	"When we are alone he act as if I am the only woman alive."	That is because she is the only woman within groping distance.
11.	"We are living together until we get married. Three years is not that long."	They are living together until he finds a fresh girl to clean house and perform services.
12.	"He doesn't believe in marriage."	At least not with her.
13.	"He can't help himself. He had a hard life."	He won't help himself. It's her turn to have a hard life.

There is a very intriguing part to the life of Mr. Abuse. He sometimes crosses the line where his girl friend or wife will finally put her foot down. If deep down he actually likes her, he will try to make amends through a paltry gift of flowers or an apology. If she accepts it, then it is back to the same old routine.

The odd part comes if she holds out. This further rejection, an unknown experience in his life, can break him down to a pitiful, sniveling creature. He returns on his knees, a sobbing pathetic mess, his vulnerabilities laid open. Although she has always thought a display of vulnerability would be a breakthrough, he loses that image of indifference, mystery, and challenge. She sees this broken form of what abused her and loses all respect and interest. The effect is much like a formerly male cat after a fateful visit to the veterinarian. Still, this situation does not happen often, and some think not often enough. No matter what you think of a Mr. Abuse, this is the guy that gets women effortlessly.

MR. ABUSE THEME SONGS

1. *To All The Girls I've Loved Before* — Julio Iglasias & Willie Nelson
2. *I Didn't Mean to Turn You On* — Robert Palmer
3. *You're So Vain* — Carly Simon
   (Mr Abuse likes to laugh at this one)
4. *Bad to the Bone* — George Thorogood
5. Anything by Frank Zappa

MR. ABUSE EQUATION

Mr. Nice Guy + Flowers + Love Notes + Mr. Abuse's Girlfriend = Mr. Abuse's Girlfriend

NOTE: For those not proficient in math, this means Mr. Nice Guy, Flowers, and Love Notes have a value of zero.

MR. ABUSE BIGGEST FEARS

1. Palimony suits
2. Burning beds
3. Common Law
4. "Her husband"
5. She finds out he is a carrier

Now that you know the three types of guys, let's return to our protagonist, Mr. Nice Guy and his temporary partner, Mr. Average. If you are a woman, you should realize that there is a lot of untapped talent out there. You need to learn how to utilize it. Many men may see painful reminders from the past or present.

CHAPTER 4

How To Scope Out And Use A Nice Guy

Nice Guys are a great asset. Whereas most women won't take a second look at one, the smart ones collect them. A woman shouldn't brush aside such opportunities. Nice Guys trust women, like women, and will do anything for women, just like a puppy dog. So don't waste this talent. Nurture it and use it. But to use a Nice Guy, one must first be able to spot one. A few hints follow.

Instructions for Scoping Out and Using Nice Guys

1. **A guy opens the door for you and does it naturally without any expectations.**

   This is a good sign, although not conclusive, that he's a Nice Guy. If he does this at a bar, he's probably good for a few free drinks. He at least deserves further study because he shows potential. If a real heart throb arrives on the scene do what comes natural. Drop the Nice Guy like an old dress.

2. **You receive a card from a guy. Not just any card, but a drippy one. "Snoopy" cards are an especially good sign.**

   This is definitely a Nice Guy or at least a Mr. Average who has fallen for you and turned into a Nice Guy. This guy is like a big fish, just waiting to be reeled in, scaled, and fried. He's good for a few dinners, plays, etc. Is your car broken? He'll fix it. Do you need some boxes moved? Give him a call.

3. **You receive a dozen roses from a guy for no apparent reason. If the guy seems nervous around you then you have a definite kill.**

   Take this guy to the cleaners. He's good for at least a couple of free dinners if he's not too boring. Don't choose any old cheap restaurant, go for the primo, overpriced French restaurant. Remember, roses aren't cheap; this guy parts with his money easily. Just mention the restaurant as a place you dream of going. The reservations are as good as made.

4. **A guy is trying to make inroads with you, although he knows you've had a boyfriend for a long time.**

This Nice Guy is a *"fill-in."* He likes you so much he will gladly play second fiddle just to be around you, always harboring the hope that one day he will be number one. The sad fact is; he never will be number one.

If you and your boyfriend don't get out as much as you would like, this is the guy to fill-in for the dull spots. He can be used to take you places your boyfriend won't take you or can't afford.

5. **A guy you see at work has an obvious interest in you and seems to be afraid to ask you out.**

This guy is considered the *"Expense Saver."* Get him to go to lunch with you. If he grovels for the bill, great! There isn't a reason in the world for you to spend money for lunch again. If he's not around very often, call him about "business" just before lunch. Mention a restaurant you're in the mood for. Continue this routine until he's trained to ask you to lunch on his own.

It is preferable that he doesn't work close to you since he could become a nuisance and lurk around your desk like a street cat. This can be resolved by having him fired for sexual harassment.

6. **A stranger stops to change your flat or fix your car, ruining his clothes.**

What a sap. You would never do the same for him. He just begs for abuse. Given his lack of value for his clothes he will obviously waste loads of his hard earned money on you. Let him.

7. **A guy is coming in from out-of-town to see you and the trip is far out of his way.**

This guy is hooked, and what is more, you don't have to see him that often. Of course, it is your duty to show him the town since you know it so well. Make sure he brings his credit cards.

Once spotted, don't let this Nice Guy loose. Here are a few additional uses for him. Be creative, there are infinite possibilities.

Other Uses for Nice Guys

1. Do your parents dislike the guys you date? Do the guys you date have no interest in family gatherings, weddings, etc? A Nice Guy is a warm body who can keep the family at bay. Bring him to the family get-togethers. Has Aunt Beth been riding you about meeting a "nice man?" Use Mr. Nice Guy as the facade. She would die if she met the guys you *like* to date. Mr. Nice Guy will be glad to do it as long as he thinks it's a real date. Hit the town with the guys you really want.

2. Tell the Nice Guy how much you love flowers. He'll send them and you can use them to impress your friends, decorate your room, or make someone interesting, jealous.

3. When your boyfriend brushes you off, if you are lonely, or just need to get out, go see a Nice Guy who is enthralled with you. Tell him how mean your boyfriend is and how you came over because you feel so "comfortable" with the Nice Guy. Prepare yourself by looking in the weekend section of your newspaper to find plays and restaurants to suggest to the poor sucker when he takes the bait.

4. Nice Guys will actually show up to help you move, paint your house, or polish your car. Take advantage of it. They even bring their own beer. The guys you really like would never show up. They have better things to do.

5. When you accept a date with a Nice Guy, make sure he calls you a day before the date to verify that you can make it. That gives you a few days to wait for a better offer. In addition, it alleviates the trouble of calling Mr. Nice Guy to cancel. He will actually be doing that for you! His call also serves as a reminder since the date will probably slip your mind anyway.

6. Always say you're sorry when you cancel on plans. This little pittance keeps this poor sap on the hook. He actually believes you. This is amazing since it may involve eating a pair of tickets as well as blowing his weekend.

7. Nice Guys have desirable friends. If you spot him with a guy you want to meet, suddenly show undue interest in the Nice Guy. (You know the routine, you've probably done it before.) Be cute and coy and then ask to be introduced. The other guy, seeing you show interest in a Nice Guy, knows you must be available. After getting what you want, you can continue ignoring Mr. Nice Guy until you spot him with another prospect.

Once you master this art, you can develop a clientele of Nice Guys. It will look somewhat like a harem. You will be going out to lunch free, your car will always be clean, polished, and running, and you will become knowledgeable about all the best restaurants, plays, and events in town. It is a great life although the juggling can be tiring.

Men reading this chapter are cringing at this point. Nightmare memories are being revived. You've planned dates and gotten the rug pulled out from under you, moved furniture while supplying the beer, sent flowers with hardly an acknowledgement, or played second string while the real boyfriend takes a leave of absence. You missed the warning signs and failed to act on them. The next chapters are for you.

CHAPTER 5

How To Tell If You Are A Nice Guy

How does a man know when he is only a Nice Guy or has temporarily fallen into that pit? There are many telltale signs. Men should heed the warnings or be trounced mercilessly.

You Know A Woman Considers You A Mr. Nice Guy...

— When she wants your deepest advice on romance problems.
— When after seeing her for several months, she gets pregnant and it could not possibly be yours.

- When her parents look forward to you coming over.
- When her male dog doesn't see you as a threat.
- When she invites you to church and others in for coffee and then breakfast.
- When after knowing her for months, taking her out, and spending money on her, you find she still isn't available for things that are important to you such as graduation, promotions, birthdays, or your funeral.
- When she thanks you for the roses but slips and calls you the wrong name.
- When she invites you over to play Scrabble because of your vocabulary.
- When her dad calls to invite you over.
- When her dad calls to invite you over, you accept, and she looks surprised to find you there, but not pleasantly surprised.

- When Guys call **you** to leave messages for her or to ask where she is.
- When after your undying devotion, you slip up once or get mad at her for using you and she finds that to be "the last straw."
- When you look in her photo album and you find pictures of relatives, mysterious men, cats and dogs. Everybody but you.
- When she goes on road trips and vacations to everyplace but your town because it was "too far and expensive."
- When she remembers her dog's birthday but forgets yours.

- When Christmas arrives and she shows you the *"neat"* gifts she has gotten for other guys, but you receive nothing.
- When none of your phone calls get returned unless she needs you to do something for her.
- When, over a candlelight dinner, at your expense, she begins asking personal questions about the availability of your best friend.
- When her father doesn't wait up when you take her out.
- Anytime she uses any one or a combination of words such as NICE, SWEET, CARING, DEPENDABLE, or GENTLEMAN when complementing you.

These are bad signs but there are many hidden messages you can detect merely from conversations with the girl of your dreams. Take a look below and see if any set off warning bells.

Nice Guy Translation Guide

SHE SAYS...	SHE MEANS...
"You are such an Angel."	"Devils are more fun."
"You are so sweet."	"You are just like one of the girls."
"You are so understanding."	"You are so easy to turn down."
"Maybe some other time."	"If I don't have anything better to do."
"I like guys that are shy."	"I LOVE guys that aren't."
"You say the nicest things."	"You say all the things I wish a real boyfriend would tell me."
"You are so considerate."	"You are considerate of me no matter what I do to you."
"Don't be like the other guys."	"I need a break from sex."
"I don't know why you put up with me."	"I really don't, but if you're willing to take it I'll dish it out."
"I love the flowers."	"I love flowers from anyone."
"What a nice guy."	"You are a leper." (See also gelding, eunuch)
"Don't ever change."	"You are so easy to use."
"You treat me much better than my old boyfriend."	"That is why he was my boyfriend and you are not."

SHE SAYS...	SHE MEANS...
"You are so easy to talk to."	"I will tell you all the things I won't tell a real boyfriend."
"I feel comfortable with you."	"We're like brother and sister."
"I don't feel threatened by you."	"You are pathetic. You loser."
"You are such a good companion."	"And so is my dog Rover."
"I do not think we should be doing this. It will ruin a good friendship."	"I would rather be attacked by a complete stranger."
"You are like a brother to me."	"And that is how I will kiss you."
"You are my best male friend."	"I have no sexual interest in you whatsoever."
"I trust you."	"How boring, why don't you lie to me?"
"My parents think you are great."	"But then, who wants someone their parents approve of?"
"I like you because you are intellectual."	"You are more fun to talk to than to mess around with."
"I feel so safe with you."	"I wish I were with someone who had no respect for me."
"We have so much in common."	"Except I don't have romantic interests in you."
"You are such a gentleman."	"I like to use you."
"You are the only one that really treats me with respect."	"You obviously know very little about me."

CHAPTER 6

Traps A Nice Guy Should Avoid

A Nice Guy has difficulty changing his ways because it's his nature to treat women well. That's his Achilles Heel and is why women prefer going to bed with a complete stranger than to go on a date with him. If you're a Nice Guy and want to reduce the amount of rejection you must endure, there are a few simple rules to follow.

Rules For Nice Guys In Bars

1. Rule number one is don't look for women in bars. The Nice Guy paradox is that they go to bars to meet the type of women that rarely go to bars. If you frequent bars, remember that a rejection in a bar is rarely a loss.

2. You did not follow Rule 1 and attempt to ask a girl to dance. She looks you over once and sees you could never ruin her life. She says, "No, I would rather not." OK. So it's embarrassing and you feel rejected. Don't say "I don't blame you." This also goes for asking a girl on a date.

3. Don't bother talking to a girl that is a "Regular" at a bar. She is usually a hardened veteran, and is definitely not looking for a Nice Guy or she wouldn't be there. For those who don't know what a Regular is, it is a person who is considered a fixture at the bar. The bar they frequent is home turf. Pity the fool who approaches her in her territory. These women know all the lines and most of the guys. A Mr. Abuse does well with these veterans and they usually deserve each other.

4. If you do get a date with a bar Regular, don't ever accept her request that you take her to that bar on the date. She is using you for a ride and a bank roll. For your trouble, you will play second fiddle to every other guy at the bar.

Nice Guy Rules For Dating

1. If a girl wants you to call a day before a date to confirm it, she is hoping for better. If she backs out at the last minute she found better or thinks doing nothing is a better option. Ditch her, it's hopeless.

2. If you need a date to something important, women can sense it. It's like a horse; if it senses you are afraid it, will throw you.

   NOTE: If you are desperate, forget even trying. I theorize that a computer listing is circulated to women with men's names on it who are desperate for a date (the Prom, office Christmas party, New Year's, etc.). To accept a date from this computer list means banishment from the sisterhood. Only circumstantial evidence can be found to prove this theory, this being that when a guy needs a date the most is when he has the most trouble finding one.

3. If you must send flowers to a woman, don't let her guess who sent them. Your name will be the last she thinks of, and also the most disappointing.

4. A woman you are interested in gazes into your eyes and says, "You are such a Nice Guy." Pick up your glove, bat, and ball and go home. You have just found another "friend," "buddy," "pal."

5. Never give a girl something she really wants unless she is madly in love with you. Wanting the object is a challenge; if it comes too easily the fun is over and so are you. Look around. You are surrounded by women who stay with men who give them nothing.

6. Don't kill yourself over a woman to get her attention. Your funeral will occur on a day she is busy washing her hair. Shooting someone else to get her attention has obvious side effects (Reference - John Hinkley).

CHAPTER 7

What Is A Nice Guy To Do?

You are with a girl and have begun to realize that you are just a pal, a buddy, a NICE GUY. Then she says something like, "You're so sweet." Don't just stand there and take it. Insult her right back. Use some of these comebacks. She will respect you for it.

Responses For Abusive Statements By Women

SHE SAYS...	YOU SAY...
"I like guys who are sensitive."	"So what."
"You are so understanding."	"What do you mean?"
"Maybe we can do it some other time."	"You ask me next time." Note: Just in case you don't know already - She won't.
"You are such an Angel."	"Go to Hell."
"You say the nicest things."	"I lie a lot."
"You are so considerate."	"This lunch is on you, isn't it?"
"I don't know why you put up with me."	"It's purely for physical reasons."
"You treat me much better than my old boyfriend."	"He probably knew you better."
"You are so easy to talk to."	"What's that? I'm sorry. I wasn't listening."
"I feel so comfortable with you."	"That's a relief. I thought you knew about my police record."
"I don't think we should be doing this. It will ruin our friendship."	"What friendship?"
"You are like a brother to me."	"You mean, like from the better half of your family?"
"I trust you."	"You do? Then strip!"
"My parents think you are great."	"I wish the feeling was mutual."

SHE SAYS...	YOU SAY...
"I like you because you're so intellectual."	"Thanks. By the way I have tickets to the Championship Wrestling match. You want to go?"
"We have so much in common."	"I thought I had more class than that."
"You are such a gentleman."	"Excuse me, but your bra strap is showing and the food stuck in the corner of your mouth is making me sick."
"You are the only one that really treats me with respect."	"I was raised to be respectful whether the person deserves it or not."
"You are so sweet."	**Sorry, this is the kiss of death. There is no proper comeback for this one.**

Now for guidance on some familiar situations that confront you. It's time to take a stand. You might be a Nice Guy but you don't have to let women walk all over you. The following list serves as a starting point. Learn from it and build on it.

1. When a woman consistently gives you a "maybe" when asked out, she must not be excited by the prospect or she's hoping better options come along. Think of it this way: A woman calls and asks you out for dinner at her expense. She will pick you up and bring you home. All you have to do is get ready and begrudgingly give a kiss at the end of the night. Are you going to say MAYBE? Hell no! ➤

    Tell her you need something more definite and will call back if you can't find another date. With luck she will be left with nothing to do and will assume she was replaced. Remember, if you can't get another date, don't call her back because you'll get turned down flat. Calling her back shows desperation. There is no mercy for that.

2. If a girl you are dancing with acts as if she is trying to ignore
    you, scopes out the dance floor, and carries on conversations
    with other people, she must think she is doing you a favor by
    gracing you with her presence. Return the favor. When she is
    completely distracted, sneak off the floor. Grab a beer and
    point out the loner dancing on the floor to those around you.
    Watch the look on her face when she realizes why she is
    getting all the attention.

3. If you make the mistake of bringing a date to a bar she frequents and you don't see her unless her glass is empty, wait until she is in the middle of a group of admirers. Run in, look her straight in the eye and say, "Someone told me Herpes is NOT curable. You lied to me!" Then storm out. She may not ride home with you but then no one else will be taking her home either.

NOTE: Dream on Nice Guy. You would never do this. It's not in your character. The least you can do is tell her you have to leave early. She will probably stay, thereby shortening your trip home. The negative aspect is that you will miss out on the sensual goodbye wave at her door.

4. The girl you are so attracted to talks to you only when you are with a friend she has primal urges for. After she finishes her cute, coy performance for the benefit of your friend, tell him she's available and easy. He'll know what to do.

5. You have dated a girl for a long time and have finally realized you are merely a Nice Guy in her eyes. She is taking you for granted. Begin taking her to less special events such as bowling, demolition derby, or miniature golf. Choose someone else for more expensive events. Eventually she will get the needed feeling of inadequacy and will gain interest in you.

6. After suffering abuse for a number of years, write a book about it. You may as well get paid for the abuse you've endured.

Perhaps these actions will cause a woman to give you less consideration than before. In that case it was hopeless from the start. You can always console yourself with the fact that she is probably attracted to Mr. Abuse types. Don't worry, they will make her pay.

CHAPTER 8

Reprogramming The Nice Guy

Let's say you're a Nice Guy. You now understand the situations to avoid, and know comebacks for offensive remarks. What you really want to know is how to make yourself attractive to women. But, it's a very confused market out there. You don't understand why women aren't attracted to you. The term Stockholm Syndrome makes no sense. You think, "How can a nut like Charles Manson get women to kill for him when I can't even get a woman to accept a date?" Think about this – A woman killed herself for a sickly, mass killing, lunatic named Hitler. For you, it seems as if the only women who would kill themselves over you are those who would rather die than date you.

Obviously Mr. Nice Guy, you are doing it all wrong. Successive failures make this self evident. Rightly or wrongly, as a male, you are placed in the position to be the aggressor. No woman is going to ask you out and you are a miserable failure at getting a date on your own. The first step is to learn how women operate, and there is no better teacher than a Pro, Mr. Abuse.

We'll start with a classic example found in a movie made in the 1950s called *The Picnic*. It stars William Holden as a wanderer who stows away on a train and gets off in a small town. The heroine is played by Kim Novak, the home town beauty queen, who is dating a rich, somewhat stuffy boyfriend. By the end of the movie, the wanderer is forced to leave town because the police are after him. Being an ambitious, visionary man, he decides to go to a big city and find "a job." This is the future he urges on Kim. Well, who in their right mind could turn that down? So Kim decides to leave her family to follow him. Her mother protests the decision.

MOTHER:
"He's no good. He'll never be able to support you and when he does have a job he'll spend it all on drink, and after that there will be other women."

DAUGHTER:
"I know. But Mom, you don't love someone because he's perfect."

Kim runs off with her eyes wide open, leaving her Home-Town-Beauty-Queen position and rich boyfriend behind. Odd, you say? Didn't James Dean play these aimless parts? He still has a following of women well after his death. What was the big turn-on for Marlon Brando when he's typecast into parts such as in *A Streetcar Named Desire* and *The Wild One* ? A remarkable number of beautiful, sensitive women attach themselves to useless, abusive men and hang on for all they're worth. It's time for them to hang onto you, Mr. Nice Guy.

Women's Traits You Can Use

Each woman has at least one or more of the following traits. These traits can be used to your advantage.

A. SELF DEPRECIATION — Women are self depreciating to an extreme. Their minds are like steel traps, storing every negative comment said to them. Remarks on looks are especially effective. Ask a woman what is wrong with her looks and she'll give you a list. Her actual attractiveness has no bearing on the length because this list accumulates from birth. It includes all the negative things said to them by their parents, boyfriends, brothers, and sisters as well as comments of teachers and strangers. The gaps are filled in by the woman's own observations.

Why is this trait useful? It's because if a man accepts her for what she is or goes overboard to get her attention then she thinks the man's a fool. How can she take him seriously if he can't see all her faults and imperfections? The feeling of inadequacy is addictive. Abandonment, being ignored, or unloved are necessary feelings for this woman. That is why a dinner at a Trucker's Cafe with Mr. Abuse can be more impressive to a woman than a date to a fancy restaurant with Mr. Nice Guy. With Mr. Abuse, she must try her best to overcome her faults and imperfections so that she can deserve to be taken to a nice place. To take a woman to a romantic restaurant at a moment's notice means you are either a pal or have no taste.

B. NEED-TO-TAKE-CARE-OF — The second trait to learn is the need-to-take-care-of or the maternal instinct. As girls grow up, men who can't take care of themselves become the post-adolescent doll. How many women do you know who live with men who can't hold a job, don't control their temper, are unstable, or are constantly in trouble? That's why you read about women who become pen pals with prisoners and later either marry them or provide money for their retrial. Typically they are repaid by getting dumped.

The message? Your worst faults can be an asset. Nurture the worst side of you. Be forewarned, if she manages to cure you of your most despicable elements, she will dump you and find another problem child. When things are running smooth, when there are no conflicts, life is good — that is when a girl friend or a wife thinks things need to change. So fatal flaws are a must.

C. MARTYRDOM — Many women have a need to play martyr or need constant conflict, otherwise life becomes boring. Ever hear women complain about their husband or boyfriend saying, "He doesn't seem to care" or, "He is undependable." The distinction is that these are complaints about their "boyfriend" or "husband" not "former boyfriend" or "ex-husband." Does she leave him? NO! She talks about it and hangs on. Soap operas make millions using characters women

can identify with who get dumped on constantly. The lesson here is: "Women aren't happy unless they are unhappy."

Comments from a professional Martyr.
1.   "He needs me."
2.   "I'll stick it out."
3.   "I can take it."

Its time for **you** to be cared for, Mr. Nice Guy.

D. CHALLENGE — A man must be a challenge. "No Win" situations are the best; married men, men with girl friends, gays, workaholics. The more taken you are, the better. That's why it is easier to get a date when you're already attached. Men cheat on girl friends or wives only because of the large supply of women who aid them in that endeavor. Always remember, no woman wants a man that would have her.

Relearning Character Traits

Beginning to see the point? You have your positive qualities all mixed up. Bad qualities are still bad qualities but not always with women. You'll now begin reprogramming. Below is a dictionary of personality traits to learn from.

ALOOF — This trait makes a man seem independent or distant. The challenge of breaking through the disinterest, to make the man attentive and feeling is intriguing. Aloofness can be interpreted as nonacceptance thereby feeding the inadequacy needs of some women. If you have little substance, be aloof. Cats are aloof. They leave home, they're choosy about their food, and women love them. (Synonym - Indifferent)

ANGRY — As in "hating-the-world" type anger. The James Dean syndrome. Look what it did for him. This trait lights up the needs-help sign. Women are desperate to help cure this anger. If the anger is turned on her, then she gets the added thrill of martyrdom and inadequacy. Ever notice that troublemakers typically have girl friends?

EGOTISM — (Exaggerated sense of self importance) We all hate egomaniacs right? Wrong. If this were true, half of all football players would never find a date. Was Mohammed Ali lonely?

CHIVALROUS — (Marked by honor, courtesy, and generosity) Chivalry, if not dead yet, soon will be. It turns off female inadequacy, martyrdom, and need-to-help motivation. It is therefore amply unrewarded and if Darwin's theory is correct it will be bred out of men. Most men will support the position that chivalrous acts have had little affect on their attractiveness.

CONFIDENT — It's good to have confidence but it's worthless to women unless it is in the right form. A man can be a mental case and a failure at everything, but if he is confident with women, he can change his bedpost to sawdust carving notches in it. Astrology, metaphysics, body language and any other magical but useless assistance take their rightful place in oblivion as confident males plow through women.

CONSCIENCE — (Consciousness of the moral right and wrong of one's own acts or motives) The most successful of the Mr. Abuses lack a conscience. The trashing of a woman must be accompanied by the inability to care that one does so. This prevents any hesitation of doing it to the next one. Lack of conscience also serves as a drawing card. Women want to help him learn that he should care and will extract microscopic signs of caring and declare them a breakthrough. What a challenge!

GENTLEMAN — Women like gentlemen to be around as long as it doesn't develop into anything serious. A gentleman makes a good butler, not a lover. A statement heard often about a gentleman is, "He is such a gentleman, why doesn't he have a girl friend?" The question answers itself.

GIVING — A man who is giving is generally rewarded with a woman that takes. Eliminate this urge. It won't get you laid. Where's the challenge in a man that gives? How will giving make a woman feel inadequate?

GOOD LOOKS — Believe it or not, this is not a necessary quality. Take Henry Kissenger, Dustin Hoffman, Woody Allen, Mick Jagger, Rod Stewart, or Bruce Springsteen for instance. All have been termed "sexy" by women. A chivalrous, giving, dependable, good looking man doesn't come close to their attraction. (It's an admirable quality that looks are not an overwhelming attraction for women and it's a benefit to all of us slugs.)

IMMATURE — A turn on for the "needs help" type of woman. Immaturity begs for a mother figure. Signs of this include a temper that blows up for no reason, selfishness, and inability to carry on a relationship.

INADEQUATE — Occasionally a useful trait. Inadequacy can be useful if a woman accepts it as a reason for a man doling out abuse. His abuse is only seen as a sign of his feeling of inadequacy. A load of garbage of course, but useful when used correctly.

INATTENTIVE — A quality that both drives women crazy and grips them. If you aren't "Scoping out Babes" while you're with a woman then you are too easy. If you always listen to her than you aren't a challenge. You get your cake and eat it too with this quality.

INCONSIDERATE — This is a common complaint used by women about their "Boyfriend" or "Husband," therefore it is not a negative quality.

IRRESPONSIBLE — Seemingly a bad trait and given as a very frequent reason for final divorce of a man, therefore it must have good holding quality. She married him, didn't she?

KIND — (Pleasant nature, sympathetic) Similar to giving and vulnerable. Kindness is readily received by women but rarely returned in kind to the giver. Martyrdom, challenge, and the need-to-help instincts are turned off. With kindness how does the feeling of inadequacy have a chance? Mr. Abuse provides kindness in minuscule amounts and has much, much more success.

MONEY — Money is the great equalizer. If you are gentlemanly, nice and considerate, without any of the prescribed attractive qualities, having loads of money is a way out. Some women are drawn to it, many will tolerate you if you have it and spend it on them. Prepare yourself for what happens if you lose your portfolio. A Mr. Abuse has no need for money to attract women.

MOODY — A quality that leads to constant, painful changes for a woman. Moodiness gives the woman a needs-help jolt regularly as she tries to take care of the mood swings. It gives an additional bonus of constant conflict in her life. Unpredictability and possible loss is addictive.

MYSTERIOUS — This is a Remington Steele-style image. The reality will never meet up with the imagination. This trait takes in several others such as moody, indifferent, aloof. The lesson here is that if you have nothing else to offer, than be mysterious. (Extreme Example: Charles Manson was mysterious - women killed for him.)

NICE — Need anything be said for this useless, waste of time, zero quality? Hide this trait at all costs.

PASSIONATE — Only good if the passion is spread among many. Passion that is freely given makes the inadequacy and fear-of-loss meter go crazy. If passion is won too easily and not shared with others then there is no challenge and no girl friend.

PERSISTENCE — This is a romantic quality where a man pursues a woman even though she gives no encouragement. It's seen repeatedly in romantic movies with the hero getting the girl in the end. THIS IS NOT THE MOVIES HERE, WE ARE DEALING WITH REALITY. Give it up. Thousands of roses are massacred daily in this futile effort.

RESPONSIBLE — What use does this serve? Does it make a woman a martyr, give her the feeling of inadequacy, or make her want to save you? Drop this quality if you are stricken with it.

POWER — The ultimate aphrodisiac. This comes in many forms: money, position, brute force, fame. How a person gains power is unimportant. They could deal drugs, lie, cheat, steal, or even kill. You will be forgiven for your sins as long as you have power. (Examples - Politicians, crime bosses, etc)

RUTHLESS — Lets call it the J.R. Ewing Syndrome. Bad as it is, behind every ruthless man (Hitler, Jim Jones, Manson) there are women who will do anything for them. It makes the needs-help-and-love meter go off the scale. Once the edge of ruthlessness is lost, so is the woman.

SHY — Some men can be insecure with women until they get to know them, or are just not the life of the party. Women will not, (and I repeat) will not search for men with this quality. The song *"He's So Shy"* is the Star Wars of reality. You hear women like men who are shy. It's true but the word emphasized is "like" not "are hot for." No doors are destroyed by the onslaught of women competing for a shy man.

UNDEPENDABLE — A constant complaint about a bad boyfriend or husband. The key words again are "Boyfriend" and "Husband." This quality turns on all four desires of women. A woman can become a martyr to this problem or take it as a sign of nonacceptance. The lack of this quality is boring and unchallenging.

UNDERSTANDING — When a man is understanding with women, it means he understands when they won't go out with him, he understands when they must cancel plans, and he understands when he is dropped for another man. Actually he really doesn't understand. Understand this: the more understanding you are, the more you will have to understand.

UNFAITHFUL — Women say they hate men that are unfaithful. What is ironic is that there is an endless supply of women for these men to be unfaithful with. Women attracted to this get the triple whammy. They feel inadequate, are given martyr status, and feel the reason he is unfaithful is because he needs their love even more. A man who is already taken reeks of challenge. The definition of unfaithful means a man has more than one partner, which makes the unfaithful man at least two up on a Nice Guy.

UNHAPPY — Ever see a very unhappy man with a woman that constantly tries to make things better? A pair made in heaven.

UNLOVING — A sign of a dead-end prospect and therefore devastatingly effective. It sends the needs-help needle to the moon. A woman will spend her life trying to extract caring from this man while giving the ax to any man who cares for her.

UNSTABLE — A great source for conflict in a woman's life.What excitement, what a challenge; martyrdom here she comes.

UNTAMED — The Don Johnson, goes-it-alone quality. Definitely a challenge. How many pregnancies occur as a way to force a man to settle down? Of course this method, when used to tame him, causes his loss. (Synonym - "Wild Man", "Crazy Man")

CHAPTER 9

You Can Be A Mr. Abuse Too

(Or At Least Fake It)

The Mr. Abuses of this world get the action. Nice Guys don't. Mr. Abuse fools around on his girl friend or wife and her friends can't wait to take her place. He's the reason for the songs *He's So Vain* and *Leader of the Pack*. If you are in the Nice Guy's shoes, you know you can't lick him so you have to join him. If you can't join him then fake it.

Lesson One - The Wrong Way

As a first lesson, see if you can find what is wrong with the following picture.

This guy is a hard core Nice Guy. He violates all the rules. Look at him. He most likely owns the house. This means a steady job, a person who takes responsibility and plans for the future. You can bet he has life insurance. What a turd. Notice the car. Inexpensive, not flashy, good gas mileage, good resale value. What a bore. He doesn't deserve a girl friend or even a dog. He even keeps his yard neat which is considerate of neighbors and also means he doesn't have anything better to do (Interpretation - No Girlfriend). Let's look inside his home.

What a laugh. Look at the picture of his parents on his dresser. He actually likes them. Who is going to feel sorry for that? He has furniture and it's not even Roman Emperor style. The bed looks like it has had little use. Is that surprising? He obviously has no character. Read on, these mistakes are easily cured with deprogramming.

The following picture is of the man on a date.

This drip has taken a woman to the best restaurant in town. She looks bored, so she must not be worried about the tab. The evening drips of romance but only for him. He's a fool who burns his money. Even the waiter thinks he's a sap. All of this must change.

Lesson Two - How To Be Irresponsible/Wild/Untamed

You want to be in demand. First you must eliminate the boring side of you. Then you need to learn how to give the impression of being wild.

A. TRANSPORTATION

To be desirable you must own a car that is not practical. In other words, you must give the impression that you pour all your money into four wheels and risk it daily in rush hour traffic. Toyota Corolla and Nisson Sentra's are banned. It has to be a car that you wouldn't buy if you were married. Remember the old adage, "Women marry a man hoping he'll change, men marry a woman hoping she won't." Either a woman must plan to make you get rid of it or she must be impressed by how she will look in it. Desirable cars are:

1. Corvette
2. Mercedes Sports
3. Jaguar XJS
4. Ferrari Testerossa
5. Jacked up Monte Carlo

Convertibles in any one of these is the kill. Being seen in the car and having her hair blown in the wind is important.

There is a problem. Maybe it is difficult for you to risk your life savings on something that depreciates faster than the monthly payments. An option is available. Buy an old Corvette. They're not overly expensive and they increase in value as they get older. Never reveal that the car is an investment or you will look tame or even worse, RESPONSIBLE.

Motorcycles are even more effective because you can provide a woman with the feeling that you will kill yourself on it. If you don't like motorcycles, buy one that's been wrecked and put it in your garage. Talk about the great wreck you had and about all the pins in your legs and plates in your head. Talk about getting it fixed so that you can "haul ass" on it again. She'll become convinced that only her love will save you from impending death.

B. LIVING ARRANGEMENTS

Never buy a house! It's far too responsible. If you own one, hide the fact that you own it. There are ways. Below are cover statements.

1. "My parents own the house and gave it to me to live in. Once it gets trashed out, I'll get them to fix it." — This is highly impressive since you not only are living off your parents but you are destroying the place too. This shows good qualities of irresponsibility.

2. "I am house sitting for friends who moved to Europe. They're going to be mad when they see how I've trashed it." — Again, it is important that you "trash" the place, otherwise you look as if you are considerate. The impression that it is temporary shows that you are a wanderer and hard to tie down. It gives that necessary sense of impending loss that will add meaning to her life.

3. "I am living here because the owners don't want to move in yet. I used to own it but I got so in debt from my cocaine habit that I had to sell it to pay the cost of going through the Chemical Dependency Unit (CDU) a 3rd time. It's really going to be trashed by the time they move in." — This is highly professional. Not only have you changed the fact that you own the house but have thrown in a drug problem and irresponsible behavior. She is really going to want to save you. (Other reasons for selling the home — Embezzlement trial expenses, fired from job, gambled away the money, etc.)

The lesson here is to rent an apartment. Besides, once you become desirably abusive, you won't have time to deal with caring for a home.

C. EMPLOYMENT

A good job is a negative. True Mr. Abuses live off their girl friend or wife. When asked why you took your current job, don't tell her it's because of better money, better opportunities, and better conditions. Tell her it's because you punched out your boss, got caught stealing, got zapped on a drug test, or got caught with the boss's wife at work while taking drugs. She'll be bowled over by your untamed, irresponsible behavior.

If you have a good job and work long hours, don't tell her it's because you like it. Convince her you're a work-a-holic. This will make her want to be the savior that makes you desire to return home. Choosing to work late rather than seeing her provides the neglect necessary in her life.

D. DRUGS AND ALCOHOL

Alcohol is not illegal and therefore less exciting than drugs but still effective. There is nothing like getting drunk and demolishing a country and western bar to get noticed by women. These guys always have girl friends. I'm not suggesting you do this, but the image of self destructive alcoholic behavior, even if a ruse, is useful. Stories about running over three school kids in separate incidents and "God knows how many cats and dogs," will generate concern and make her want to protect you. Be especially sorry about the third kid since it was your little brother. Back up your ploy by running over her cat. This image of self destruction caused by your drinking problem will make her mother you as she tries valiantly to save your life. She is now your slave. Who says co-dependency is a negative.

Drug problems are really in vogue as evidenced by the number of businesses built around curing the addiction to them. The "Just Say No" campaign is making a serious dent in the coolness of this trait, so use it while you can. Periodically call a woman and babble about strange and disjointed topics. If asked, deny you're messed up. She will be right over to do your will.

It's a given that drug dealers get women. It's part of the reason they do it. The other part is for the money which again brings you back to doing it for women. Explanations that the women are only attracted to the free drugs or the excitement doesn't console a Nice Guy who can't find a date. The problem is that becoming a dealer or a druggie is a high price to pay (Example — Jail terms and the type of dates you get in prison). You must at least give the illusion that you are experienced in drugs. Here is how.

1. **The illusion of being a former dealer** — Living in this type of company requires cover stories and clothes like Don Johnson's in *Miami Vice*. You aren't a dealer so giving the impression you used to be one is impressive. Good stories follow.

a. "I've got to be cool now, one of my contacts in Washington told me that the DEA has my name on their list." — It's really cool to be so BIG that you are noticed by the DEA. Only a wild-man could be endowed with such an honor. Women will go crazy over you.

b. "Going back to the joint a third time would mean life." — Another cool sign is having been in jail. This story will make the rounds and everyone will want to be your friend. Having never been in jail is not impressive.

c. "I saved all my money, bought my dear old mother a new home and retired. I'm out of the business. It's too danger-ous, and most my friends are dead." — The former life of danger and excitement and your impression as a wise old dealer will make the women want you. Characterize any scars you have as scars from bullets, switchblade cuts, etc.

2. **The illusion of being a heavy user** — The one problem associated with this ploy is that you will constantly be offered something. If you aren't "Cool" and don't do drugs there are ways to avoid them. The above explanations are useful lead-ins as to why you can't take anything. Others follow.

a. "I'm sorry. No coke for me, I have to let the skin graft in my nose heal."

b. "I don't do that stuff anymore. I like PCP." This is really cool because PCP is a crazy-man's drug. One minor problem is if someone has some to offer. You answer, "I only trust it if it's from my own lab."

c. "I'm already high, I don't want to waste it." This isn't impressive but it will get you by. (NOTE: Hogging down drugs is more impressive and will get compliments of, "Boy were you wasted last night," and "I've never seen someone take so much and live.")

Although women who travel in this crowd are either idiots, don't have much class, or both, they are generally loose. For a guy that can't get a date, it's better than nothing.

E. THE DON JUAN ILLUSION

Your effect on women is exponential to the number you are already involved with. If you are not involved then there is no challenge, no impending loss, no conflict in her life, and therefore no interest in you. Listed below are ways to make a woman feel that you are hard to hold.

1. Slip up occasionally and call her by the wrong name, then claim ignorance to where the name came from.

2. Forget to pick her up for a date. Then give an excuse for not being there. (Think of one that will make her think you're lying.)

3. Have a woman with a sexy voice make your phone recorder message. Every woman calling you will have to listen to another woman answer your phone. This drives them crazy with desire.

4. Your address book should be loaded with women's names, so add fake ones. Women are curious about address books. If there aren't many other names then she'll want to remove hers. Adding stars next to names is effective. To be devious don't put stars next to the woman you like. She will realize she still hasn't earned a rating.

5. Buy sets of earrings and spread them around (under the seats of your car, the couch, the bed, in the bathroom, etc.). Your excuse to a woman who finds them is that your sister used your apartment for a while. She won't believe you, thus not only have you received the positive attribute of being loose but also a liar.

F. POOR CHILDHOOD

This is a good source for generating concern and also provides a universal excuse for the abuse you give her.

EXAMPLE — "My dad beat me, my mother beat me, my grandmother beat me, my dog hated me, and my sisters tried to sell me on the street but no one had any change."

This background will provide an excuse for why you were unwillingly forced to fool around on her, why you yell at her, or why you forget to show up for a date. She will accept the excuse and take it upon herself to do anything to make up for all your past neglect.

Lesson Three - How To Criticize

A compliment lasts for ten minutes with a woman. Criticism lasts forever, so give a woman something that lasts. I'm not talking about diamonds.

A. BEGINNING CRITICISM

There is an art to criticism so begin slowly. Remember, you're a Nice Guy. This runs against your grain.

Since women bank information on all their faults, they like to talk about them to see if others agree that they're true. Here are examples of how to respond:

1. She says, "I think I'm gaining weight." You say...
    a. "Its not that noticeable." (You have noticed which to her means she has blimped out.)

    b. "No. Not at all." (Pretend you don't believe what you're saying. The thought that it's so bad you have to lie will devastate her.)

    c. "I like full figured women." (She'll think you are putting the best light on the situation because you feel the condition is terminal.)

2. She says "I don't like my hair this way." (She is either fishing for a compliment or is worried that it looks bad in public) You say...
    a. "Maybe the air is too humid." (Translation — her hair freaked out on her).

    b. "I hardly noticed." (This will make her think it is a major distraction to everyone she comes across and will become a major subject of discussion as well as a media event.)

    c. "I think it would look better with a hat." (This to her means it is so bad she needs to hide it.)

B. ADVANCED CRITICISM.

Once the Nice Guy has become adept at subtle criticism, you can become more blatant. It's at this point that it has full effect and will make her your slave as she will do anything for you to make you change your mind.

1. She says "I think I'm gaining weight." You say...
   a. "I don't think I should be seen with you. Call me when you've lost 15 pounds." (A comment like this will make her go anorexic)

   b. "You look like my fat aunt." (Not only have you told her she is fat but that she also looks old. This is a form of "slam dunk.")

   c. NOTE: To be truly blatant you should have noticed first and called her Miss Piggy. The lesson here is never hesitate to point out inadequacies.

2. You pick up your date and she looks ravishingly beautiful. You look at her and say...
   a. "Are you ready?" (You know she's ready but to her you told her you can't tell.)

   b. "You're going to go out wearing that? Well, we don't have time for you to change. Let's go anyway." (The rest of the date is shot for her. Her self image will be of a witch. In addition, she owes you for allowing her to be seen with you.)

   c. "I decided we're going to a pool hall so don't wear that." (After she goes through the trouble dressing up, it's all wasted. This shows you were totally unimpressed.)

C. STIFLING COMPLIMENTS

The Nice Guy must gain control of his reactions. There are times you will instinctively want to compliment a woman. You must catch yourself before the mistake is made. Pictured is an example of a man who has not gained control. The second picture shows a Pro in action.

WRONG

RIGHT

D. GRAB BAG OF CRITICISM

There are literally thousands of ways to criticize a woman. Whether the criticism is valid or not is not the point, as long as SHE thinks it's valid.

1   **APPEARANCE** — Only maximum effort put into her appearance is acceptable (Not worthy of a compliment but merely acceptable). Anything less is grotesque. Complaints on looks can run the full gamut — She is too fat or too thin. Her hair is too short, too long, the wrong color, doesn't look right, too thin, too thick. Her shape is not curvy enough, too flat chested, too curvy. Her legs are too fat, too thin, too short, too long (RARE), too muscular, has cellulite (Always Effective), are shaped like fence posts. Her feet are too big, too small, funny looking. Her hands are too big, feel like shark skin, smell like her feet.

2.   **PERSONALITY** — Personality traits considered good by one can be disliked by another, so all are available for criticism. Examples — "You have no sense of humor." (A comment you make after saying something no one would like to hear). She never laughs, she laughs too much. She talks too much, not enough, about nothing important. My friends don't like you, are bored by you. She has a bad temper, not enough of a temper.

3.   **OTHER FORMS OF CRITICISM** — Ignoring a woman translates in her mind to being inadequate. Showing up late or forgetting to show up provides a needed jolt of disinterest. Never allowing her to meet your parents or friends shows you are embarrassed of her.

As one can see, criticism is limitless in opportunities and fun. Compliments will become important later in the process. They are to be doled out sparingly as a carrot on a stick to keep her blindly following, always hoping for just one more small sign of acceptance. Compliments are also useful to build her for a big fall. Men string women along for years using these methods.

Lesson Four -
Our Reprogrammed Hero

The scenes that follow have been changed to show the new and improved Mr. Nice Guy. First is the scene at his house.

Now here is an attractive man. He has the right clothes, a flashy looking car, and the wrecked motorcycle to show the crazy-man in him. There is an obvious need for someone to help him mend his ways. He couldn't possibly own the house because it's well trashed. (Merely cutting the grass, replanting and cleaning will bring back its value - A small price to pay to attract women.)

Now lets see his bedroom.

A slight modification of his parent's picture emphasizes a bad family history and the room looks well used. Drug paraphernalia, empty beer cans, old pizza box. What a cool dude. It will be clear to a woman that the man that sleeps in this room hasn't found the woman who can tame him. She will sacrifice herself to be the one that does.

Here is our Hero on a date.

This is a man that has what it takes to get women! No explanation need to be given.

CHAPTER 10

The Incurable Nice Guy

What about the incurable Nice Guy, who just can't help himself?
Try as he might, he can't be abusive. Just when he gets the girl
interested, he does something stupid like compliment her, or send her
flowers, or show up for a date on time. If you are hopelessly affected,
what can you do?

Professions For The Incurable Nice Guy

1. **BECOME A PRIEST** — This eliminates having to give
   excuses for not being able to find a date. A Priest's success
   rate with women is similar to yours. Negative Aspect — Since
   your position restricts you from women, some women will be
   turned on by the hopelessness and challenge of mastering
   you. Now that the opportunity presents itself, you can't do
   anything about it.

2. **BECOME A EUNUCH** — Similar to the above option
   except an operation is required. You still won't be able to get
   dates but now you won't care. Negative Aspect — The operation. It is suggested that massive quantities of pain killer be
   administered.

3. **BECOME A SHEEP HERDER** — You will now have
   companionship. Negative Aspect — Sheep can't cook.

4. **JOIN ANTARCTIC EXPEDITION** — Positive Aspect —
   Penguins are better looking than sheep. Negative Aspect —
   They can't cook either.

5. **JOIN THE NAVY** — You are off shore so much, what difference does it make if you're a Nice Guy? Submarine duty is the best option. It is suggested to avoid dropping your soap in the shower.

6. **JOIN THE FOREIGN LEGION** — This is like the Navy but gets you more exercise. It also gives you opportunities to vent your frustrations if you are lucky enough for a war to start. Negative Aspect - See above warning on showers.

7. **WORK IN A WOMAN'S PRISON** — Who knows? Maybe even you can get lucky there. (NOT!)

Dating For The Terminally Nice

If the above options are too extreme then another option is to revamp your selection of dates.

1. **DIVORCEES** — Many of the best looking and vibrant women marry early. They married early during a time when they were uninterested in your type and bagged a Mr. Abuse. Once they can't take anymore of the drinking, joblessness, undependability, amorous behavior of their husband, they divorce him. About 50% learn their lesson and are interested in a Nice Guy. The other 50% wish they were still being abused by their former husband or look for someone who will. Negative Aspect — In the event of marriage, you will be the one to play daddy for the kids abandoned by Mr. Abuse.

2. **MAIL ORDER BRIDES** — Due to starvation and strife in their countries, these women are desperate enough to settle for you.

3. **EXCESSIVELY UGLY, FAT GIRLS** — The question is, are you desperate enough?

4. **ORIENTAL WOMEN** — For some reason, being nice, dependable, and responsible are not considered undesirable by this culture.

5. **DATE MEN** — For Nice Guys it is far easier to get a date with a man than with a woman. Taking this option will cause some women to take on the challenge of changing you back. Negative Aspect — You probably won't like it, you will lose your friends, and your parents will disown you.

6. **WOMEN OVER 30 WITHOUT KIDS** — So you have lived though Elementary school where girls wanted to date High School boys. You got into High School and now girls your age want Seniors. You are a Senior and they want to date College Students. You finally get to College and now they prefer College graduates. Now they reach their 30s and don't have kids. The clock is ticking. They are on the last leg of their child bearing years. Suddenly a Nice Guy becomes an option. It's payback time. You can either run with it or date younger women because now you have money and time is on your side.

CHAPTER 11

What Have You Learned?

Has your life changed? Have you absorbed any of this? It's time to find out.

1. You have $200. You want to spend it on ...
   A. A lifetime subscription to *Mad Magazine*.
   B. Flowers and dinner for two at a good restaurant with a "dream girl."
   C. A new CD unit for your stereo.
   D. A subscription to *Hustler* magazine and the rest on beer.

2. You spend money on a girl because ...
   A. Mom told you to.
   B. She deserves it.
   C. It's expected.
   D. She forgot her credit card.

3. After the third date, she still gives you a peck on the cheek. You think she is ...
   A. Too forward.
   B. Sweet and innocent.
   C. Messing around with someone else.
   D. INSANE. The second date would never occur.

4. Women are attracted to men who ...
   A. Have a nice mommy.
   B. Know how to treat them well.
   C. Have money and intelligence.
   D. Don't treat them the way they want to be treated.

5. **The words "Date and Relationship" ...**
   A. Are unknown
   B. Are rare but desirable.
   C. Are desirable
   D. = SEX

6. **Her reply to your request for a date: "Dinner and dance for Saturday? Call me in a couple of days, I might be able to make it." You say ....**
   A. "Really! I'm going to tell all my friends I got a 'MAYBE'." (And you do)
   B. "I promise I will call." (And you do exactly that)
   C. "Sure, I'll call." (And you don't)
   D. "Are you insane? YOU call me, but only if you can afford the date. If I don't have another date by then, I might, and I repeat MIGHT let you go."

Now score as you did before with all "A" answers being 0, "B" = 1, "C" = 2, and "D" = 3. Reference the groupings below for your score.

Score 0-3 Mama's Boy

You're hopeless! Give up.

Score 4-9 Nice Guy

You sap! Can`t you learn anything? Either reread this book and try again or reference chapter 10 for options.

Score 10-15 Mr. Average

You're still a potential sucker. You'll have to try harder.

Score 16-18 Mr. Abuse

Congratulations. Now get out there and ruin some lives.

Conclusion

For women who have read through this book and interpret it as too negative toward women, I can only say that much of it was written for the humor of it (Some of the more embarrassing Nice Guy situations, regretfully for me, weren't invented). If you remember anything, remember that if a man doesn't treat you well now, you can only expect worse later. Pay attention to a man's actions, don't live on your perceptions. Men are cut and dried, they are what they are. They are not clay to be molded, not filled with deep inner emotions just looking for a woman to dig them out.

Take a look at a Nice Guy. Sure, he's an easy kill, but the grounds are already littered with divorced women who managed to nail down the most popular guys. Besides, once his confidence with you builds, he may become that undependable, amorous, insensitive S.O.B. that will make your life exciting.

As a closing fantasy to Mr. Nice Guy, imagine this: The girl who you were so good to returns for comfort after the Mr. Abuse she ditched you for, ditches her. She wants some attention to build her ego. You turn to her with as close to a Clark Gable look as you can give and say those famous words…

"Frankly my dear, I don't give a damn."

It wasn't until that moment that Scarlett really appreciated Rhett Butler. The scene is a classic and still gives women hot flashes. The combined effect of rejection and indifference will make her want to have your babies. The problem is that you can't go back because then the effect is lost.

The message to be learned by Mr. Nice Guy: get that lonely, puppy-dog look off your face. Forget the sensitive, castrated, modern man tact. The desirability of that was invented and has no place in the real world. You know what the problem is? You don't think you're good enough and it shows. A man who is total scum can sweep a woman off her feet just by having the right attitude. So you are more than enough already and all the new-age, astrology, crystal, bullshit out there isn't going to add a thing.

Always remember, if a woman has an interest in you, she will make the effort to show it and you won't need a magnifying glass to find it. If it is abuse you are receiving, cut the ropes yourself and look at the positive side. With your success rate, you'll always remain a spectator to all the new and fashionable STD's[1] that spring up on the market.

1 — STD's (Sexually Transmitted Disease)

DO YOU HAVE A STORY TO TELL?

Sharkbait press is accumulating your tales of woe for a possible new book. The stories are limited to 500 words or less. Subject areas and examples follow.

I. Biggest Jerk Stories
   A. For Men - "The biggest jerk I was ever dropped for..."
      " The most successful womanizer I ever knew..."
   B. For Women - "The biggest jerk I ever dated..."
      "I was always amazed at how this jerk attracted women..."

II. Get-even Stories
   A. For Men - "I finally turned things around by..."
   B. For Women - "I got even with a jerk by..."

III. Nice Guy Stories
   A. For Men - "I treated this woman like a queen and in return she..."
   B. For Women - "The nicest eunuch, I mean guy, I ever knew..."

Please note that you must have a good sense of humor about these stories. We don't want any whiny, crybaby stories that make people sad. If your story is selected and the book printed, you will receive a free copy of the new book and $15.00. Stories are due by December 31, 1994.

Please send your story, address, and phone number to:

Nice Guy Stories
Sharkbait Press
P.O. Box 11300
Costa Mesa, CA 92627-0300

About the Author

Marcus Meleton is a sometimes writer, who works as an engineer in Southern California. He was born in Shreveport, Louisiana and raised in Lafayette surrounded by four sisters who left him utterly confused about dealing with women but totally enamored by them.

Marcus attended college at Louisiana State University, and graduated from the University of Southwestern Louisiana with a Computer Science Degree (which he describes as, "A degree known for its rabid womanizers"). He graduated with an MBA from the University of Georgia and attends Orange Coast Community College for writing and film courses in his spare time.

His career has ranged from door to door sales during college to serving as an Air Force officer in the Pentagon. He has also lived and worked in Athens, Georgia and Dallas, Texas before arriving in Newport Beach, California, completing his Coast to Coast move through the country. During an interview, when asked about his current dating experiences, his answer was, "I surf a lot now."